Travels with Clancy

Poetry from Coast to Coast

By
Autumn Siders

Copyright © 2022 by Autumn B. Siders
Any original content may not be reproduced or used in any manner whatsoever without the express written permission of the publisher except for the use of brief quotations in a book review.

Printed in the United States of America

First Printing, 2022

Cover Photos © 2022 by Autumn B. Siders

ISBN 9781736491942

E.M. Sanchez Press
PO Box 82
Moultonborough, NH 03254

www.autumnsiders.com

Also by Autumn Siders:

#nofilter
Not My Type
She Loves Me, She Loves Me Not
Spermeo & Juliegg

<u>Children's Books</u>
E.M. Sanchez Mysteries

To all those who wander
and are not lost;
to all those who are lost,
and only need but wander.

Maggie

I was probably sixteen
when your face lit up
as I showed off my license
and you explained what's what.

Freedom awaits,
the open road is yours
whether it's a thousand miles
or just down to the store.
Blacktop for miles
and worries in the rearview
as long as your heart holds out
and the engine still turns,
the road never has to end.

1864 Mitchell Map of the United States
Map altered by the author; landscape altered by mankind.

Temperature Control

In my younger days,
it was full throttle,
the in-between
was for those
who couldn't commit.

Things move for a reason,
adjustments can be made.
A world set in stone
finds it hard to turn
when things don't fit.

What changed my mind
as the years went on
was how hot it gets
with the heat blowing
on full blast.

Luckily, I discovered
that the dial can move
and avoiding the extremes
creates comfort
that will last.

The More We Stay the Same

Golden arches and crowns
yield to castles and gold stars.
Potholes and faded lines
result from endless lines of cars.

Signs change,
speed limits range,
views bleed
from
country
to
city
to
mountains
to
plains.

Every mile ahead
offers hope of a new day.
The gas tank creeps to *e*.
The radio still plays.
When static fills the air
and it's time to turn the dial,
the same old songs will play
with each ever-changing mile.

Tilting at Turbines

Shadowing behemoths
against the pink sky.
Their red eyes blinking
as their blades fly.

Carried by the wind,
yet firmly in the ground,
may they stay in motion,
forever circling round.

Such monstrosities
some might say,
but the fight to save Her
can't wait another day.

Art Lessons in Iowa

I've never studied art;
I couldn't tell you
who painted what,
or which method was used.
I can't fill you in
on Impressionism
or why Picasso felt so blue,
but here is an impression
I can make unto you:

The sun sets
across the great plains
and a canvas is painted
as colors fill and drain.
Pinks, purples, and oranges mix
to the perfect shade
when darkness enters
and daylight fades.
Endless road ahead,
the wary traveler in awe
of a painting in nature
lacking any flaw.
Colored clouds float,
a piece of art delicately hung

until it shatters
with the smell of cow dung.

Dream Girl

Just a dream,
a dream girl,
not even my dream,
not even my girl.
I could travel the world,
I could sail the seas,
I could scale the mountains,
I could climb the trees.
But,
the truth is
I travel better

alone.

Empty Spaces

AfterDrivingThroughSoMuchEmptySpaceIDecidedThatPaperShouldntExperienceTheSameCaseIndentationsNewLinesPunctuationWhatAWasteStillIWriteToFillBecauseHumanNatureIsToCreateSomethingFromNothingAllTheWhileForgettingThatSomeSpaceIsNecessaryToGrow

Anywhere, U.S.A.

Boarded up windows,
abandoned towns,
homeless humans
with luck so down.
Cars rotted out,
streets cracked,
glass shattered,
money lacked.
Ghost towns,
haunted by greed,
left to fend,
open to plead.
A franchise
of forgotten hope
thriving on blood,
sweat, tears, and dope.

A Lonely, Blue, Metallic Box

A dying art
from a dying breed
on a dying day.

Hope diminishes
with every mile
I drive away.

A lonely, blue,
metallic box
is all I seek

to drop a line,
share the journey,
so to speak.

Sure, those wires and waves
could work faster
than archaic ways,

but still I cling
to inevitable
postal delays.

Then, like an oasis
in a desert of
data-driven trends,

a beat-up old box
awaits my missive
as this dying day ends.

Field Guide to the Wildlife of I-80

Traveled all this way
to see a simple Steller's Jay,
and I end up instead
with empty trees overhead.

While the trees did not deliver,
I'm inclined to forgive Her
since the highway became
Mother Nature's to claim.

A hawk swooping low,
a skunk, babies in tow,
a deer frozen still,
a coyote in search of a kill,

an eagle soaring above,
a roadrunner sounding like a dove,
and alas, for all to see,
on the ground, not in a tree:

the bird I've been seeking,
his crest slowing peeking,
above the brush, beside the rush
of a new habitat
in the making.

Exit 284

Everything you need,
and more
since you never know
what's in store.
Feel like a tourist
or feel like you're home.
Stay for a movie
or continue to roam.
It's not like pulling teeth,
you can travel with ease,
or even visit the dentist
if that's what you please.
A haven full of history
and memories in the making,
just a dot on the map
that's perfect for braking.

Ungodly Hours

Back home,
 I always enjoyed
 those mornings
you find yourself awake
 at some ungodly hour.
The sun has not yet reached
 the steaming cup of coffee,
the birds have not yet sung
 those morning calls to rise.
The quiet settles
 on the critters
just going to bed
and stillness blankets
 those who slumber.

It's a different calm
 on the road
 at these ungodly hours.
The truckers are the critters;
 either just settling in,
 or just waking up,
 depending on which
 roads they take.
 It leads me
 to believe

that these hours,
no matter where they are spent,
are not
        ungodly.

Rules of the Road

Always obey the road signs.
Abide by the speed limits.
Know the laws.
Buckle up.

Pay the tolls.
Only use the left lane to pass.
Check your fluids.
Check your tires.

Use your mirrors.
Always look twice.
Don't pick up hitchhikers,
even if they look nice.

Road sign on I-80 in Nevada

Emmilee Risling is Missing

Another one gone,
a statistic,
paperwork to be shuffled,
or thrown away.
A throw-away.
What did the report say?
Was she Asian?
Native?
Surely, not white.
White, we could work with that.

We would work with that.

Don't worry, we are changing the system,
you know, the same one
that failed you in the first place.
No one is gone without a trace
as long as you're a white girl,
with a pretty face.

-

Emmilee Risling is an enrolled member of the Hoopa Valley Tribe. She has been missing since October 2021.

As of 2016, the National Crime Information Center has reported 5,712 cases of missing American Indian and Alaska Native women and girls. The U.S Department of Justice missing persons database has only reported 116 cases. The lack of communication combined with jurisdictional issues between state, local, federal, and tribal law enforcement, made it nearly impossible to begin the investigative process.

In October 2020, Savanna's Act *and the* Not Invisible Act *were signed into law.*

Savanna's Act *is a bipartisan effort that intends to improve the federal response to missing or murdered indigenous persons.*

The Not Invisible Act *works to increase intergovernmental coordination to identify and combat violent crimes against Indians and on Indian lands.*

For more information, here are a few of the many resources available to those willing to look:

https://www.nativehope.org/missing-and-murdered-indigenous-women-mmiw

https://www.nativewomenswilderness.org/mmiw

https://www.csvanw.org/about-us/

https://mmiwusa.org/

McDiarmid, Jessica. *Highway of Tears: A True Story of Racism, Indifference, and the Pursuit of Justice for Missing and Murdered Indigenous Women and Girls.* Toronto: Anchor Canada, 2020.

Te echaré de menos

It's not the missing you now
that hurts the most.
It's the knowing that this feeling
will be permanent one day.
All we face right now is distance,
our love from coast to coast.
A quick chat or text will help
to keep the pain at bay.
But all those eerie airwaves,
a foreshadow of your ghost,
leave my heartstrings aching
as the future fades to gray.

Early Bird

Rising in the dark
has its perks,
no traffic, no sound,
only nature at work.
The trails are empty,
the air is chilled,
the world is waking,
morning has stilled.
A crunch underfoot,
a snap in the trees,
a soft cooing bird,
a gentle breeze.
Sunlight flows,
moonlight ebbs,
and the early bird
gets the spiderweb.

Dinosaur Hunters

Dinosaurs once roamed these forests,
or maybe, they didn't.
Dinosaurs don't roam,
do they?

Their bones won't be found
under land too sacred
to dig, to destroy.
Their remnants won't be seen
under brush too flush
to be a decoy.

But, for a moment,
on a fine spring day,
two dinosaurs roamed,
singing songs along the way.

How Much Is That Doggie in the Tree

I can hear you,
scolding me from above,
definitely not
the soothing call of a dove.

You keep hiding,
yet I can feel your eyes,
ever watchful
in your blue and black disguise.

My eyes are glued
to the tree line overhead,
looking for a bird,
but seeing a dog instead.

What tricks these trees
can play on mortal minds;
their beauty is a given,
but their mystery is undefined.

Simpson-Reed Trail in Jedediah Smith State Park in California

A closer look on the Simpson-Reed Trail in Jedediah Smith State Park

Over-Easy

We watched the sunset
together.
That over-easy egg
in windy weather.
Back east with you,
the sun already down,
out west for me,
the waves only drown
your voice on the speaker
just shooting the breeze,
sharing a friendship
that bloomed with ease.

Is Jessica Fletcher Home?

This small little town
just down the coast
has all its population
and so few crimes to boast.
Hard to believe
Hollywood made this the place
for an east coast town
with its west coast face.
Still, there sits the home
of crime solver extraordinaire,
but I highly doubt
J.B. Fletcher is there.

A Snapchat Away

In this brave new world,
family is only
a Snapchat away
as long as the cell towers
are working today.
As connected as we are,

the disconnect is clear.

It's not the distance,
but the closeness that we fear.

The Coast Is Clear

Nothing for miles
and yet, everything
exists.

Hope, promise, life, death, disaster, ferocity,
tenacity, calm, power, salty tears, infinite depth,
profound mystery, a Pandora's Box, a crashing
cacophony of eternal triumph.

We are never
out of the woods,
but today,
the coast is clear.

Another Red Panda Tail

High up in the treetops,
I keep my eye on y'all.
I think we both know
it's a long way to fall.

My excitement mounts;
your boredom evident,
but your lethargic waddle
keeps my heart content.

I'd stay perched right here
as long as you'd nap in the sun,
but those glares you give
say voyeurism isn't fun.

A Eureka moment
and I know to move along,
but with cuteness like this,
it's hard to stay strong.

A red panda at the Sequoia Park Zoo in Eureka, CA

I Can't Help Myself

I will never break my promise to you,
but sometimes I can't help myself.
I'll be out on the town
and I get feelings I cannot shelf.

It's not the same,
it's never the same.

The love in my heart
is made solely for you
and no matter the distance,
I'll always stay true.

I may have to touch,
to pet,
to console.

But those other cats mean nothing
because you complete my soul.

Top Left, Bottom Left, and Bottom Right: Cats of Blue Ox Historic Village in Eureka, CA Top Right: Cat of Woodland Villa Cabins in Klamath, CA

All
Night
Long

Trucks race by
all
night
long.

Cars rush through the drive-thru
in & out
all
night
long.

Doors slam,
toilets flush,
children wail
all
night
long.

Two a.m. arrives
and quiet settles,
eyes shut
sleep comes…

"Fuck you! Just fuck you!"
Doors slam,
cars rush,
trucks brake,
eyes open,
sleep will not come…

The expletives continue,
so I quietly close my door,
rush to my car,
and join the trucks
who have been racing
all
night
long.

Dancing Fog

I trail the storm,
ice and snow in its wake,
but the plows do their job
and I'm wide awake.
The wind blows fiercely
and the snow billows like fog,
beautifully dancing,
but throwing a cog
in my ever-rolling wheels
that have no intention to stop.
The mountains grow near
and the storm becomes slop,
the state line even closer
as the sky turns pink.
Morning is calling
and the snow
is gone in a blink.

Clancy

Are you feeling blue
now that you know me,
but I don't know you?

Are you feeling the thrill
of endless possibilities
and so much time to kill?

Are you feeling antsy?

> Like you need
> Like you want
> Like you long
> Like you live
> Like you breathe
> Like you bleed
> Like you survive

> when you travel
> with
>   Clancy.

Yellow Monster

Colors melt,
shades and hues,
we all forget
about high noon.
To set and rise,
preferable by far
than the nagging reminder
of a monstrous star.
Life it gives,
life it takes.
We travel round
the world it makes.
Are we the monsters,
or is it that ancient yellow ball
that must die an empty death
bringing darkness to all?

Ode to the Road

The heart wants
what the heart wants.
Rubber to the pavement,
a blacktop confidant.
Every day a new beginning,
every page a brand-new font.

The soul needs
the freedom to explore.
Expression running rampant,
seeping from the core
and every piston pumping
towards an open door.

The road awaits
to lighten your load,
welcoming your steel
and humble abode
and helping to forget
all the baggage you've towed.

Blowout

Sometimes, the pressure
is just
too much.
The walls can
collapse,
burst,
bust.
Rolling along,
everything is fine,
next thing you know,
you're crossing the line.

So sudden
so frightening
so expected
so enlightening.

Never add more pressure,
always check the wear,
since the weight of your travels
can catch you unaware.

Home

We both know it's not a place.
"Where the heart is," is so overdone.
The heart can roam this land
and end up empty, broken, and scarred.
If I left it, solely in your hands,
I'd forget to love and be loved back.
It's more than a feeling,
not as obligatory as a calling,
more important than responsibility,
as settled as a rolling stone.

I can go back,
or I can take it with me,
but even the thrill
of the open road
can't compete.
The mumbling words
of a bumbling poem
can't capture
the sentiment
that you
are
home.

Please enjoy a couple poems from the lovely Emilita Isabella María Santina Anna Pinta Guadalupe Dominga Rodríguez Sanchez Scroogè Siders de las Botas.

Countless Hours

I am counting down the days,
impatiently awaiting,
and oh, how my heart is aching
knowing that in that matter of time,
I must suffer,
I must long,
I must endure
countless hours
of torturous time
waiting for you
to leave.

I Ain't Missin' You at All

Has it only been two weeks?
Hardly a vacation at all.
I may have slept right through it;
I didn't hear you call.

You're coming home today?
That is hardly enough time
to find a place to hide
and cover up my crime.

Have you brought me something back?
You know I'm a fan of fish.
I didn't miss you at all,
so hurry, fill my dish!

Acknowledgments

Thank you to anyone I met along the way who found a way into these pages, whether they be *homo sapiens*, *felis catus,* or anything in between.

To the crew who held down the fort while I was away, I knew y'all wouldn't burn the store down! Thank you.

Karen, I will always appreciate you for offering me so many roads to travel. You are my family by choice.

To the Swain Family, thank you for the generous contribution towards my travels. There is a remote gas station in Nevada that will always make me think of you. And a low budget horror film.

Brittney, you know you make a wonderful sounding board. Thanks for indulging my ideas and insults. May we share many more sunsets.

My love, my life, my heart. You are my partner in every endeavor, Emilita.

And Me, no journey on this planet could ever compare to the feeling that you are *home.*

About the Authors

Autumn Siders lives in New Hampshire with the world-famous cat, Emilita. She holds a B.A. in English from the University of New Hampshire. She is the author of *#nofilter*, *Not My Type: Stories*, *Spermeo & Juliegg: A Reproductive Tragedy*, *She Loves Me, She Loves Me Not,* and the E.M. Sanchez Mysteries. She also poorly maintains the blog butwiththemind.com and is terrible at social media.

Emilita Siders grew up in the mean shelters of the Lakes Region of New Hampshire. As soon as she found two schmucks who would fall for her act, she made her furever home with them. Her work has been the focal point of *#nofilter, Not My Type: Stories, Spermeo & Juliegg: A Reproductive Tragedy,* and *She Loves Me, She Loves Me Not*. She is the inspiration for the E.M. Sanchez mysteries. When she is not writing, she cannot be found unless she is sleeping or eating. Her favorite words to rhyme are "fish" and "dish."

Bark on a tree in Prairie Creek State Park

To the Grove of Titans in Jedediah Smith State Park

www.ingramcontent.com/pod-product-compliance
Lightning Source LLC
Chambersburg PA
CBHW030312100526
44590CB00012B/604